Explore more in the Celebrating Us series:
1. Little Black Baby
2. Little Baby Bump
3. Blacknificent Me

Join the journey of love, growth, and discovery in each book.

Just Blooms

Blossom Through Adversity

ISBN: 978-1-0685033-2-0

Little Baby Bump

by O'Cheng Bloomfield

Dedication

To Khalani and Khayr, who inspire me every day with their boundless curiosity, infectious laughter, and unwavering love. This book is a tribute to you, my most cherished sources of happiness and moments of highest achievement. Be the stars you were born to be, lighting up the world with your brilliance. With all my affection, O'Cheng

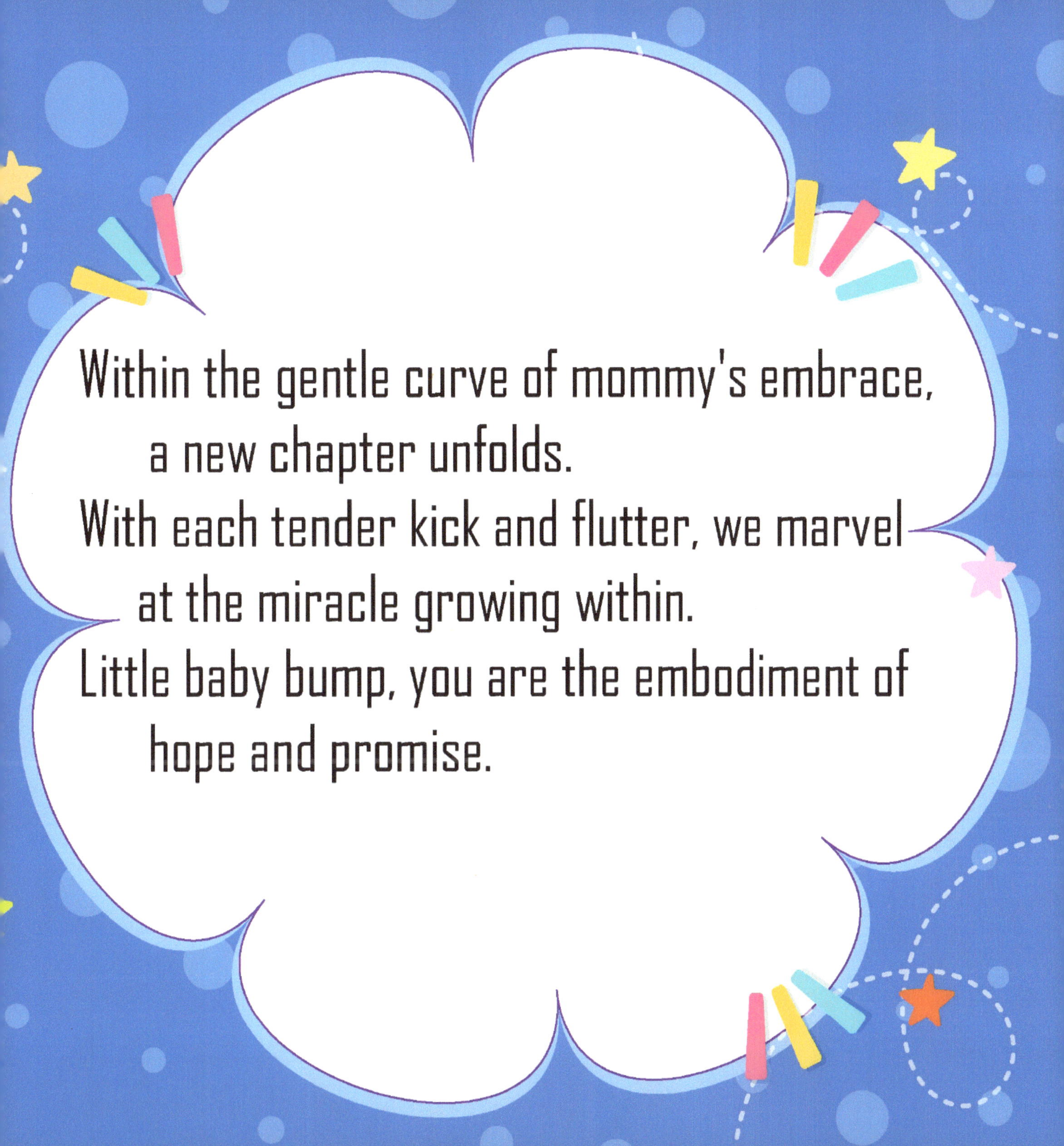

Within the gentle curve of mommy's embrace,
a new chapter unfolds.
With each tender kick and flutter, we marvel
at the miracle growing within.
Little baby bump, you are the embodiment of
hope and promise.

My mommy's tummy is swollen,
Daddy calls it a bump.
He says it's where my baby sibling grows,
Inside of Mommy's tummy, nice and snug
in a warm cozy lump

Daddy says this is how little brothers
and sisters grow,
Inside of Mommy's tummy, where love
starts to flow.
Mommy says that's how I grew too,
She showed me a picture, and I saw
it was true!

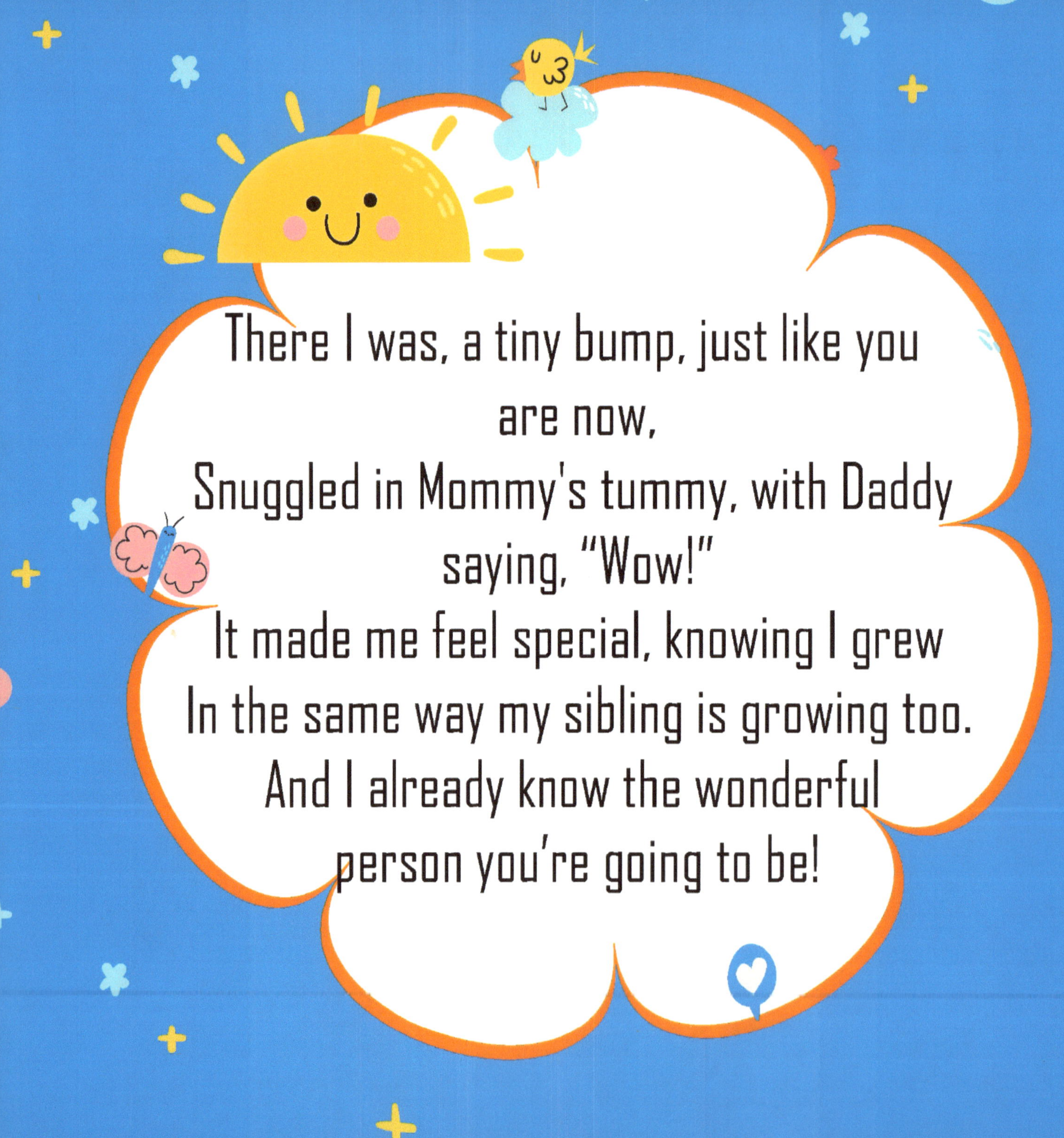

There I was, a tiny bump, just like you
are now,
Snuggled in Mommy's tummy, with Daddy
saying, "Wow!"
It made me feel special, knowing I grew
In the same way my sibling is growing too.
And I already know the wonderful
person you're going to be!

Mommy said she felt kicks and little
somersaults too,
She'd smile and say, "Baby, we can't
wait to see you!"
Daddy would listen with delight, his ear
to the bump,
Feeling each movement, every
little jump.

Daddy and I help Mommy out,
Because carrying little baby bump is a big job, no doubt.
We help to cook, clean, and we pick up the toys.
Daddy helps with carrying the shopping, strong and grand,
And I stay close to Mommy, always holding her hand.

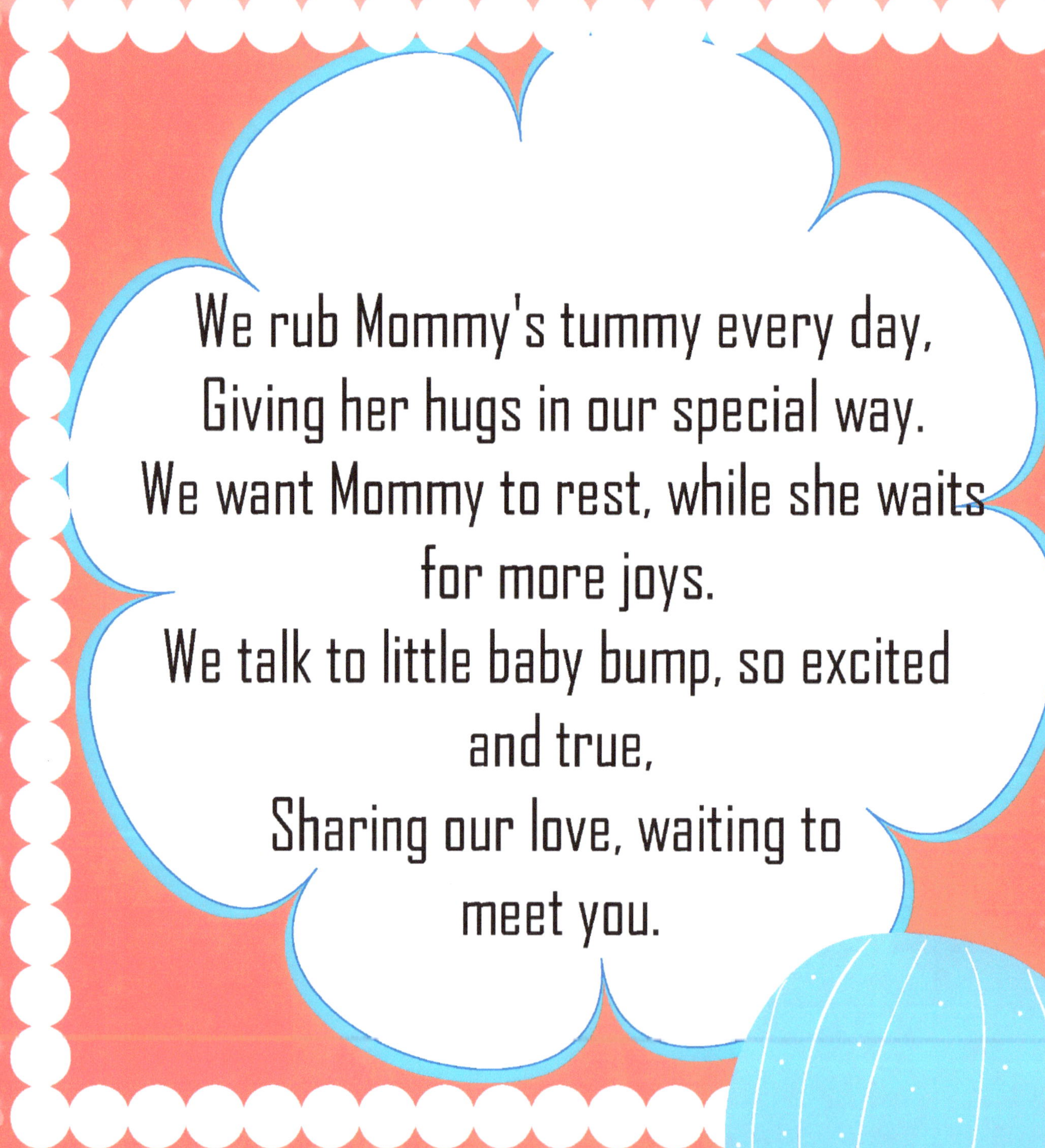

We rub Mommy's tummy every day,
Giving her hugs in our special way.
We want Mommy to rest, while she waits
for more joys.
We talk to little baby bump, so excited
and true,
Sharing our love, waiting to
meet you.

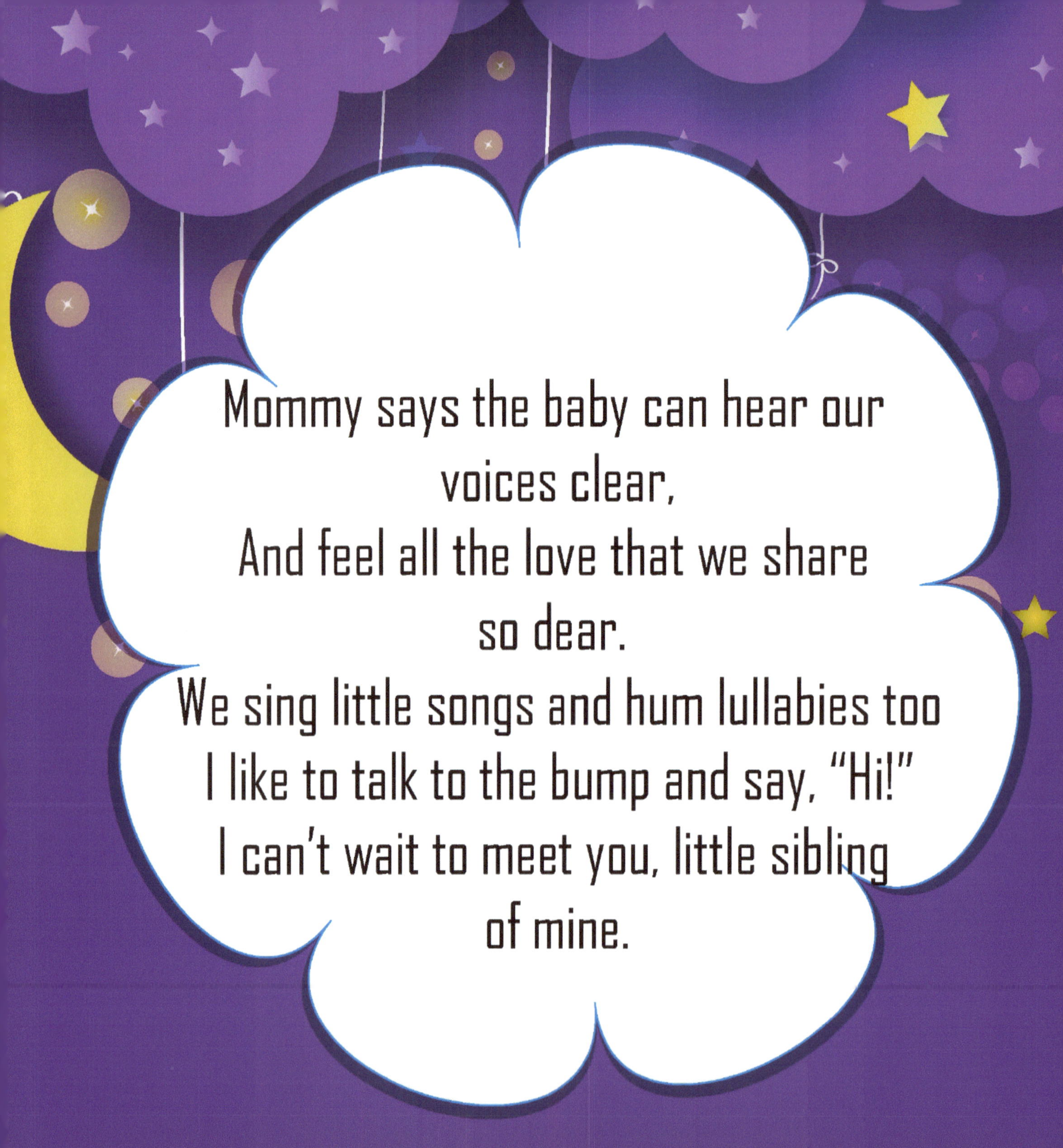

Mommy says the baby can hear our voices clear,
And feel all the love that we share so dear.
We sing little songs and hum lullabies too
I like to talk to the bump and say, "Hi!"
I can't wait to meet you, little sibling of mine.

Every day, we get closer to the day you'll arrive,
When we'll hold you and love you, and our hearts will thrive.
I'm so excited, to see your tiny little fingers and tiny little toes,
Little brother, little sister, little baby bump, I love you.

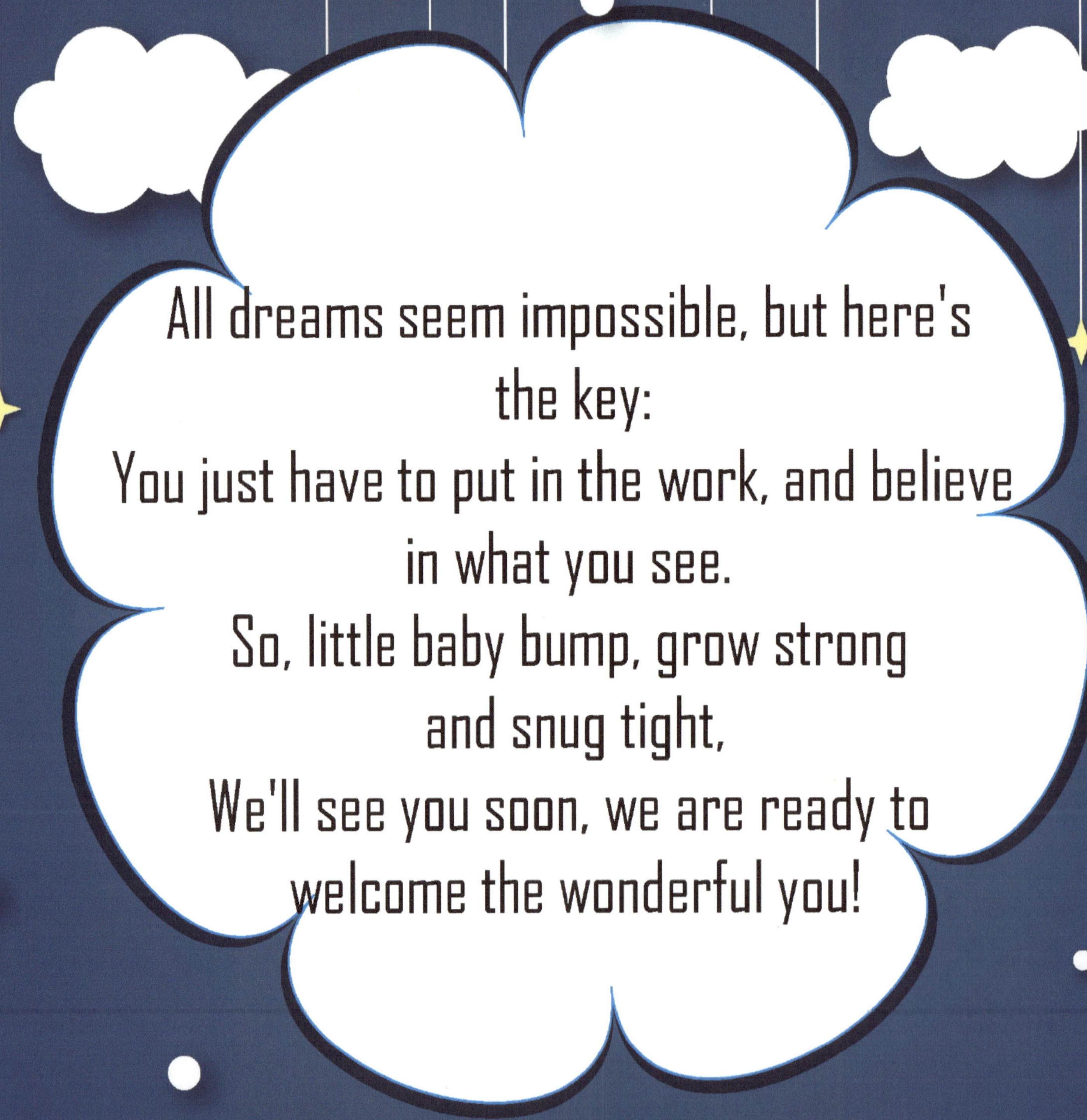

All dreams seem impossible, but here's
the key:
You just have to put in the work, and believe
in what you see.
So, little baby bump, grow strong
and snug tight,
We'll see you soon, we are ready to
welcome the wonderful you!

ALSO IN THIS SERIES:
- Little Black Baby
- Little Baby Bump
- Blacknificent Me

Discover all the adventures and lessons
with the Celebrating Us series!

The "Celebrating Us" children's book series is
a heartwarming collection of stories that shine
a light on the beauty, strength, and joy found
within every child.
Through vibrant illustrations and engaging narratives,
this series celebrates diversity, family, and self-love,
making it perfect for young readers and their families.

www.ingramcontent.com/pod-product-compliance
Lightning Source LLC
Chambersburg PA
CBHW042139030726
47599CB00002B/545